Banners of Pride

of Pride

Memories of the Durham Miners' Gala

by

Derek Gillum

Foreword

There have been many books written on the subject of the Durham Miners' Gala and the many Lodge Banners that attend this historic event held in Durham City on the second Saturday in July. This year's Gala is the 125th and also the 100th Miners' Festival Service held in Durham Cathedral. There has also been a huge upsurge of interest in former mining communities to get a new banner.

This book is different because it is written by a person who has dedicated all his time to actively promote the need to restore old banners as well as the need to raise funds for new ones.

The rich history of our coalfield and mining communities should never be forgotten. What the Gala and the Lodge Banner stands for to miners and their families is still as strong now as it was over the years when the coal industry was king.

Alan Cummings
Easington Lodge Official

Alan Cummings and the Easington Lodge Banner. On the right is a photograph of the men killed in the Easington disaster of 1951.

Previous page: Bandsmen, Lodge officials and families with the Philadelphia Banner at the Durham Miners' Gala in the 1950s. The Philadelphia Lodge was from the Dorothea Colliery in the Herrington area.

Copyright Derek Gillum 2009

First published in 2009 by

Summerhill Books
PO Box 1210
Newcastle-upon-Tyne
NE99 4AH

Email: andrew_clark@hotmail.co.uk

ISBN: 978-1-906721-10-7

Printed by: CVN Print Ltd, Maxwell Street, South Shields

The book is dedicated to George Rowe

George Rowe was a good friend of mine. He worked at Lambton D Pit and Vane Tempest Colliery. A family man, wife Marjorie, daughter Katherine, son-in-law Howard Ward and grandchildren Craig and Anna.

George and Pat Simmons were founder members of the Lambton & Houghton Banner Group. George was a great supporter of the Durham Miners' Association. He was also an extra in films and TV such as Crocodile Shoes and Our Friends In The North.

The 2008 Gala was special for George and Pat as TV star Ricky Tomlinson came up to Durham to march with the Lambton & Houghton Banners.

George was passionate about banners and mining heritage and never forgot his beloved Fence Houses where he was born. Sadly after a long illness George died on 15th October 2008. A sad loss to us all. Lest we forget.

George Rowe with Ricky Tomlinson and supporters.

George with Pat Simmons and former Deputy Prime Minister, John Prescott.

3

Memories of the Durham Big Meeting

The Durham Miners' Gala was started in 1871, two years after the formation of the Durham Miners' Association. The first Gala was at Wharton Park in Durham City. The peak of the mining industry in Durham was in 1913 when 164,246 men were employed, producing 40 million tons of coal per year.

After Nationalisation in 1947 there were 127 pits in Durham, although not all were fully represented at the Gala as some lodges did not have a banner – they did not have the money to buy one! Small Lodges such as Metal Bridge and Stanley Cottages Lodges never had banners.

The 1950s was when the Gala was at its that peak when it was estimated that 300,000 people attended each year. Some banners would be led into Durham by men in fancy dress who became well known characters. The year 1957 saw a drop in attendance by between 30 and 40 percent because a bus strike restricted travel to the trains. Not many had cars in those days.

The 1960s saw the start of the sad demise of the coalfield with many pit closures throughout the county. In 1969 it

The Vane Tempest Lodge Banner with 'The Famous View' – Durham Cathedral overlooking the River Wear.

was the centenary of the formation of the Durham Miners' Association and 25 banners of collieries that had closed were marched through the streets of Durham. That Gala was also a sad day as two miners had been killed the night before at Easington Colliery. Fourteen men were saved as they scrambled clear of a fall of stone.

The 1983 Gala saw an estimated 20,000 people turn out. One of the main attractions that day was over 100 banners displayed in a marque on the Gala field. Among the collection was the Tursdale Banner of 1893. There was no Gala in 1984 because of the Miners' Strike and a rally was held instead.

The band leads Shotton Lodge Banner.

The last deep coal mine in County Durham was Wearmouth Colliery that was closed in 1993, however in more recent years there has been a steady rise in those attending the Gala. Between 2000 and 2008 there have been a number of Banner Groups set up in villages throughout the county to raise funds to have new Banners made.

In 2008 there were more banners at the Gala than there was in 1960. Long live the Gala.

Here are three pictures from the Gala from the 1990s.

The band takes a break in front of the Mainsforth Lodge Banner.

The Byers Green Lodge Banner is paraded.

Blackhall Lodge Banner with the slogan – Leisure Through Modernisation.

When Coal Was King

Without mining there would have been no Gala. Here are a few images to remember the industry that played such an important part in so many lives.

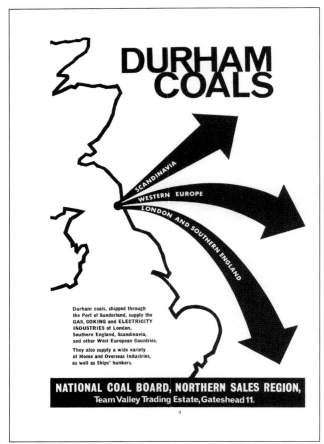

A National Coal Board advert from the early 1960s showing the importance of Durham coal throughout Europe.

Four Horden miners ready for work. Bottom right is John Close.

A commemorative postcard for the West Stanley Colliery (Burns Pit) Disaster. An explosion on 16th February 1909 killed 168 men and boys.

Right: The prize winning pit ponies at a show. Included are ponies from Marley Hill and Elemore. The animals worked hard and sometimes suffered injuries. The closure of the mines meant the end of the exploitation of ponies, many of whom never saw daylight again after being taken below.

Left: Coal hewers at Dorothea Pit, Philadelphia. It vividly shows the cramped conditions miners had to endure to make a living. The Dorothea or Dolly dated from 1816 and did not close until 1958.

Right: A coal bill from Silksworth Colliery for 1934. Coal was 75 pence per ton, in today's money. It is small wonder the miners were so badly paid.

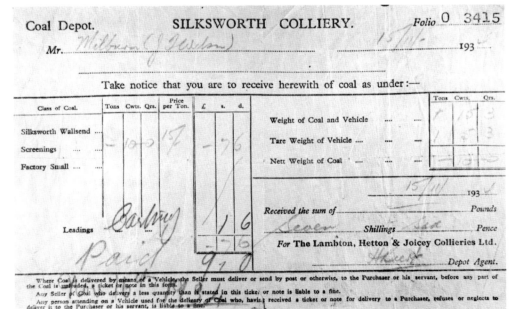

Freedom Night

Arthur Reed remembers his time at the Gala in the hard times before the Second World War in an extract from 'Our Village – Memories of the Durham Mining Communities' by Keith Armstrong.

In small mining villages during the 1920s and '30s there were rare occasions when people could throw off the yoke of the masters and forget their troubles for a while. Such a village was mine and a rare occasion was the Durham Big Meeting.

The Friday night before the Saturday, the atmosphere of subdued excitement that had built up during the week, gave way to unrestrained boisterousness that infected young and old. The working members of the family would gather at the union rooms, which was a pub, to watch the lifting of the banner. At this point, as a warming exercise, the band would play a tune. The effect of hearing the music was to send most of the young 'uns running towards the band. A crowd of shrieking, laughing lads and lasses, hopping up and down, knocking each others' caps off. We were free to go in with jerseys with holes in, short trousers (adult trousers cut down), dirty faces and legs, stockings sloggered over boots, and join the marchers.

The march had started by the time I reached the milling group behind the banner. I was grabbed by a cousin, who dragged me through the crowd of men, saying: 'Thee da's waiting for thou.' When handed over, my cousin was off to join his mates.

My dad firmly grasped my hand as I was hopping up and down like a jack-in-the-box. His first words to me were: 'Pull thee socks up and put thee cap on straight.' This I did, hopping from one foot to the other using my free hand. Looking up at him, I said: 'Are yu carrying the banner this year?'

Looking down at me he said: 'Not this year lad.' Seeing the expression of disappointment on my face he bent down and said: 'Th's gannin' to Durham.'

Gripping my hand, we jostled our way to the front so as to be walking under the flapping banner. I was surprised to see our Jack carrying the banner. I knew now how and why I could go to Durham. Sticking my pigeon chest out in pride, I walked behind the banner with my dad.

Craghead Banner and Lodge at Durham Cathedral in 1939.

Dancing in the streets at the Durham Miners' Gala in 1949.

After walking a short distance, I said: 'Dad, our Jack's wobbling about. I thought he was strong. Our Frank's helping him to keep the pole up.' Giving my arm a sharp tug, which pulled me to face him, pointing his finger at me, he said: 'Th' sees o'er much for a young 'un. He's had a drink or two, so say nowt to yu ma.'

To us young 'uns, the banner was a piece of cloth on which was painted a picture on both sides. When older, we would appreciate the art and craftsmanship that had gone into the making of the banner. The words on the banner had no meaning to us young 'uns but, in years to come, we would learn the hard way; learn also of the deaths, starvation and cruelty men and their families suffered, were still suffering at the time of these memories, so that the pictures and words would, for future generations of miners, become reality.

As the marchers moved from street to street, the older lads and lasses linked arms and zig-zagged from one side of the road to the other. They couldn't dance the full width of the street as the pavements were crowded, mostly with women, young and old, with clean pinnies or aprons. Wives holding the bairns up to see their dads, some shouting at husbands with young 'uns in tow to 'look after them'. Mothers shaking fists in the directions of sons, shouting at them not to spend all their money tonight. To be caught with your arm around a lass, unless officially courting, was trouble in the shape of a brother or the heavy hand of a parent across the lad's ear. But not this night.

Whether it was the thought of the beer waiting for them at the pub, but the speed of the marchers increased as they got nearer to the starting place, the pub, where the banner would be stored ready for tomorrow.

The excitement over, the young 'uns were dashing off home with dads, straight home or else. I hurried straight home to ease my hunger, which was satisfied with the home baked pies, this particular Friday night's treat. Then a bath and off to bed.

South Pelaw Colliery band and banner at Durham on Big Meeting Day.

A Day To Remember

Living in a colliery house, and growing up in a pit village in County Durham in the 1950s, brings vivid memories of some hard times. Throughout, these sometimes cold and hungry years, there were always days of sunshine, and it is these days that seem to last longer in the memory.

One such day was Christmas Day which was always waited for in eager anticipation. The few, but treasured, Christmas presents and the abundance of sweets, nuts and fruit made life feel good.

Another such day was that of the Big Meeting at Durham, it was so important to mining families throughout the county. Some weeks before the meeting miners would gather to select the men to carry the banner and its associated ropes with tassels. This period was the start of the excitement, knowing Durham Day was not far off. It was indeed an honour and a privilege to be selected to represent the lodge by carrying the banner and it made the whole family very proud.

Durham Day started early in our house, we quickly got dressed and washed and gulped our breakfast of porridge, before running the messages up the shop for bread and cigarettes, after which you could go out and play.

Most of the kids from the colliery houses made their way up to the Workingmen's Club, to wait outside and watch whilst the men with the banner were readied. They all formed a column with the bandmaster leading and the banner lined up behind the band. While the column moved off, miners and their families joined in by lining-up behind their banner.

The procession would march through the village, up the main road, passing the shops and the crowds of people gathered on the corner end of the rows of colliery houses. The villagers would cheer and clap as the procession passed them. Throughout the parade, children would follow alongside, skipping and jumping excitedly and pointing out their friends in the column.

The abiding memory of the procession, was the shiver down your back and the hair on the back of your neck standing on end when the band was playing. The whole event made everyone very happy and proud of the village and its pit. The parade was stopped at the cricket ground and the band, union men, the miners and their families would pile into the waiting 'trip buses' and all were quickly away to Durham, and it was still just after 7 o'clock in the morning.

During the day the village was like a ghost town. The children left behind would gather to play and the main topic of conversation was, 'When are you going to join the band?' The adults left seemed to be discussing whether or not our band was first into Durham. In those days there was a great sense of belonging, in being part of a mining community and family life was at its most recognisable with Mam always there whenever you needed her. The day soon passed and as it neared 5 o'clock the kids would make their way up to the cricket field to await the buses return from Durham.

When the buses arrived back, the band and the banner would assemble outside the cricket ground. These would be proceeded by a line of boys and girls, mams and dads dressed in cowboy hats and 'Kiss Me Quick' hats. This line would stretch right across the road from side to side with all their arms linked behind their backs.

Seaham Banner coming back from the Gala in 1956.

As soon as the band struck-up, the front line began singing and yelling with joy and happiness. As the procession moved off down the road, the line swayed from side to side and they danced and sang to the music of the band. It was obvious some of the front line revellers were the worse for wear after the long day at Durham on the beer. The line would meander across the road sometimes colliding with the lampposts or people gathered along the roadside, it would also regularly collapse but the line would soon be reformed and continue on, merrily all the way through the village.

As the procession moved down through the village, the band would play some rousing music, much to the delight of the villagers who clapped and cheered and shouted good wishes to all in the parade. Some of the bandsmen had their hats tilted to one side and their lines wavered slightly. Throughout all the proceedings the big drum kept that regular beat (with or without music) and kept everyone in step. The miners holding the banner and its ropes could be seen to wander violently from side to side, the swing being directly attributable to the amount of alcohol consumed during the day.

The procession stopped outside the Workingmen's Club where it had started earlier in the day. After forming a semi-circle around the banner, which was rested against the wall of the club, the band would play the last tune. This tune would be some poignant lament dedicated to the memory of all miners who had lost their lives in the mining industry.

Invariably, with the music over, all bandsmen and banner men dispersed, some into the club, others were taken home by their families giving them some welcome support. The talk at home was of the events of the day at Durham, and the distribution of presents like candy rock and novelties for the younger children of the family and sometimes a present for Mam.

Those days have now faded into the past but will always be fondly remembered. It is important to recall the contribution village life, the pit, the band, and the unions made in the formative years of recent generations, it made us the people we are today.

It did not matter that you did not get to Durham, there was always next year to look forward to.

This article by Ray Card was originally published in 'Durham Coal – A People's History' by Andrew Clark & George Nairn.

Right: Hylton Colliery Silver Band and various members of the Miners' Union, outside the Castletown Welfare Hall around 1955.

Hylton Colliery Silver Band was formed in 1949 and disbanded in 1979. The band are standing, left to right: Herbert Cope, unknown, Jim Taylor, Jimmy Brownless, Robert Taylor, Chris Surtees, Leslie Bell, John Haley, Dennis Brownless, Ray Reid, W. Archibald, Tommy Burgess, Jim Elland, Jimmy Farrel, W. Archibald Jnr, Bill Baharie, Bill Craggs, Teddy Ward, George Graham, Gilbert Crossley, Ron Snowdon, Jimmy McDermitt, Maurice Woodmas and John Graham. Seated, left to right: Teddy Walton, George Cope, Jimmy Anderson, James Wood, George Scott, Harry Brown, Harry Graham, George Vickers, Tommy Golightly, J. O'Neil, Councillor Bowmaker, George Scott, George Clarke, Walter Wilson and James Brownless.

Leaving For Durham

Left: The local miners' lodge at Eldon parading outside the Royal Hotel, Close House before their trip to Durham for the Miners' Gala of 1913. The banner appears to be the old South Durham Lodge one of red and orange damask silk with a purple blue border.

Right: Seaham Lodge Banner marching by Seaham Colliery on the morning of the Durham Miners' Gala in the 1970s.

Left: Thornley Banner marching around Thornley Village on the morning of the Gala in 2003.

Big Meeting Day

Stanley historian and author, Jack Hair, recalls his memories of Big Meeting Day.

My dad worked at East Tanfield and the biggest event of the year was the Durham Miners' Gala held in Durham City. Each colliery had its own miners' lodge affiliated to the DMA.

At the local meeting of each lodge, they would draw out the names of those men selected to carry the banner into Durham. There would be two men on the poles and four on the banner strings. Six men would carry the banner in and out of Durham. Only fully paid-up union members were allowed to carry the banner.

Some collieries like Craghead, South Moor and the Morrison and others had their own brass bands. Others would hire a band in for the day. It was the custom for most collieries to parade in their own villages before travelling into Durham. Several of the local Stanley pits would march either up or down Stanley Street before they made their trip into Durham. East Tanfield used to meet at the Empire Club, Stanley. Because it was a special day, drinks were allowed. The band were always sent over to the Co-op Cafe for their early morning breakfast and then it was time to go. Buses had been hired in for the men and their families. Once in Durham our assembly point was the Garden House pub. The brightly painted banner was taken out of its bag and placed over the poles. The men lined up. The band first, followed by the banner and officials and behind the banner were the miners and their families. The banner was a symbol of that particular lodge and there was a great feeling of pride and affiliation to your pit and banner swelling up inside you.

The scene as you went down under the railway arches was staggering. There, waiting, were tens of thousands of people lining the streets, all the way down to the bridge at the bottom of Silver Street. Up above were the Castle and Cathedral, and even these went unseen amidst this grand spectacle.

Band and banners at Lower Front Street, Stanley around 1962.

Cadets lead the way for the Bearpark Banner outside the County Hotel in the 1960s.

On one such day, as we reached the bottom of Silver Street, everything came to a halt as the bands ahead were unable to move any further. These narrow streets were filled to capacity with not a spare inch to move. The bands were still playing and the crowds still singing and the different tunes ran into each other until it was difficult to separate one from the other.

Slowly, we struggled up this street before turning to go down to Elvet and see the politicians of the day on the balcony of the County Hotel. At this point the crowds were like a sea of people, no beginning and no end. With the politicians were other dignitaries and invited guests. Some bands would stop there and play a special tune thus holding up the following bands and banners.

Eventually we reached the top of the bank leading down to the Sands Racecourse. This view was also spectacular. The whole area seemed covered with people, bands and banners. It was possible to hear at least ten bands before you and as many following on.

Once we reached our designated area, the banner was set down against a fence and the band instruments placed in front of it. The banner carriers could at last take off their carrying straps and have a well earned rest. Many would go off to the nearest pub, while others sat where they could for a meal with their families and friends. During the afternoon, the remainder of the lodges and their banners continued to make their way down to the racecourse. Many people went down to the riverside to have a row on the boats. Meanwhile the politicians gave their speeches from the raised platform and could be heard all over through the loud speakers dotted around the course.

Many of the fairground shows that had been to Newcastle Races had made the journey to the Gala and a good time was had by all. One of the years that my dad carried the banner, Mam had bought him a new white shirt for the occasion. With temperatures soaring and the task of carrying the banner, he sweated profusely. This was still the days of the tin bath and the sweat brought out the coal dust from his pores and his new shirt was stained in coal dust sweat. He was so proud of carrying this banner.

Some of the banners and lodges had been up to the Cathedral for a service. By the time the last lodge came down on to the Course, it was virtually time for the first to have arrived to lift the banner and head back up the steep ramp to head back through the city. Some of the banners were edged in black. This signified there had been a death or deaths in that colliery. Once, Easington Banner was almost totally draped in black due to the disaster there in 1951 when 83 miners lost their lives.

The journey out was even livelier due to the merriment and drink during the day. Many of the younger people would link arms almost the width of the road and dance side to side down through the narrow streets. It was a time of celebration. I know how proud I felt, walking just near my dad, in the shadow of the banner that he was carrying. He and his colleagues represented their lodge, their pit and their town with great pride and dignity. In 1949 they had won the Production Banner, the first ever awarded, and Dad was drawn to carry this banner.

Eventually the bands would reach the area near Dryburn Hospital where the buses were waiting for them to return home. On arrival at Stanley the banner would be unfurled once more. The banner men would again raise it to the sky and, following the band, would march up Stanley Street amidst great cheers from local people. A grand day!

Many years previously my Grandfather Hair, also a miner, had been to the Gala. He didn't normally drink but that day was an exception. On arriving home, some men came to my gran's house and asked her for the piano. Apparently, while at Durham, he had sold it to some of his friends and had failed to tell her.

One of the best bands I ever heard at Durham was in 1960 when Tanfield Lea Colliery engaged the 751 United States Air Force Band. This band was a marching and counter marching band and even counter marched on parade while still playing. They too, played in Stanley before going off to Durham where they had a rapturous welcome. The people of Tanfield Lea definitely danced in and out of Durham that day. American Ambassador, J.H. Witney, attended that meeting at Durham and forecast the winner of a horse race later that day – and it won!

The band also gave a performance for the local people over that weekend at Murray Park, Stanley. Long gone are those heady days, even though there is still a Miners' Gala. Though still popular, it has lost some of its meaning now that the coal mines no longer exist and the miners no longer employed. All that's really left are the memories.

The Burnhope Banner and Band at Durham. A man on the right is holding a sign advertising the Herald – the pitman's newspaper.

Stories from the Banners

Every banner has a story to tell here are a few.

Wearmouth Banner showing the cancelling of the yearly Bond by Mr Roberts in 1869. The bond tied a miner to a colliery and made it impossible for men to leave and seek work elsewhere.

The Willington Partnership Banner showing the former collieries in the area – Brancepeth, Sunnybrow, Oakenshaw, Willington, Page Bank and Bowden Close.

Right: Leasingthorne Lodge Banner. The Banner proclaims that 'Health is Strength' and has a portrait of Conishead Priory Convalescent Home in Ulverston. The Priory had been bought in the late 1920s by the Durham County Miners' Welfare Committee and was opened in August 1930. If a miner wished to stay at the Priory, perhaps after an injury or illness, he applied to the Lodge Secretary and then his name was entered into a ballot. The lucky ones chosen would stay a week or a fortnight.

In the 1950s a brochure described the home: 'Darts, dominoes and a television room provide indoor entertainment, while outside there are facilities for bowls and putting. There are, too, organised outings to the Lakes, Blackpool and to football matches during the season … Approaching 70,000 have attended the Home since it was opened in 1930.'

The Home was closed in 1969 and is now a Buddhist Centre.

The Marsden Lodge Banner and officials in the 1950s. The Banner says 'Firm as a rock we stand' and shows the famous Marsden Rock, just off the coast from the colliery, in all its glory. Sadly, erosion by the elements has seen the collapse of the Rock's arch but the local miners were obviously very proud of their well-known landmark.

Right: East Hetton Lodge Banner. The Banner shows the Sam Watson Rest Home in Richmond. This description of the home was given in the 1950s:

'First priority is the wives of NCB employees and female NCB employees in the Durham Coalfield. Consideration can also be given to applications from the wives of redundant miners who have not taken up employment outside the mining industry, the widows of deceased workmen and in exceptional cases, justified on medical grounds, applications for a second stay at the Home.

'The Home is one where the tired or not-so-well mother can stay a fortnight and return to her household duties re-invigorated by the rest, good food, cheerful company and tonic North Yorkshire fresh air.

'It has all the best features of a first-class holiday hotel, without fuss and regimentation. Obviously, there must be some rules, but they have been kept to a minimum and are designed to ensure the smooth running of the establishment and to promote rest and the happiness of the guests.

'There are no restrictions on movement. Guests can come and go as they please, having regard of course to meal times.'

The Bevin Boys Association Banner at the 2007 Gala. In the black miner's helmet is Warwick Taylor, Secretary of the Bevin Boys Association. The Bevin Boys were called up for National Service during the Second World War. During the war, 33 ballots were held at fortnightly intervals and 20,896 men were selected to work in the pits. There were a further 4,164 who volunteered to work in the mines and 15,657 'optants' who opted for employment in the coal industry in lieu of service in the armed forces. Former service personnel totalled 6,651 and there were 41 conscientious objectors who worked down the pits.

Right: The Westoe Mechanics Banner with a portrait of this South Shields Colliery. Local author Andrew Clark was in Shields the day the winding tower was demolished in the early 1990s. He recalls:

'The area round the pit was packed with spectators to witness the demolition of the tower by explosives. The man who pressed the button to set off the explosion had won the honour in a charity raffle. Many of those who gathered that day were former miners and all of them were sad to see another pit be lost to history. One said to me, "This is a sad day for the whole of the North East." Another told me, "I feel sorry for the young lads – the ones in the toon. There's no jobs for them." When I asked one miner who had lost his job that year what was his future he replied, "It's as black as the coal."

'It's now hard to believe there was ever pit at Westoe. The area has been cleared and rebuilt on. I think it's ironic that a pit that was destroyed in such a way has this motto on its Mechanics Banner: 'The past we inherit the future we build'. There was no future for Westoe or any of the other pits I remember in Durham.'

Banners and Bands

Left: The Morrison Busty Lodge Band and Banner at the New Kyo Miners' Institute.

In the years after the Second World War you would see Banner after Banner with their bands and followed by members of the Lodge and their families. From throughout Durham they would travel all to attend the Big Meeting. There would be days when the Brandon Lodge had 300 people dancing their Banner into the Gala.

Right: Marley Hill Colliery Silver Prize Band around 1950.

Francis Newman of Sunniside Local History Society recalls:

'The Marley Hill Band practised in the back room of the Greyhound Inn, Sunniside. It was excellent entertainment for the customers who could listen to the band playing whilst drinking in the bar. On Durham Miners' Gala Day the band would form up at Marley Hill then march down to the front of the pub with union lodge officials, proudly carrying their banner. The band would play a few pieces before embarking for Durham City.'

Left: The Vane Tempest Banner with Malcom Smith, Lodge Official at the 2008 Gala. The Pittington Band leads the way. Today the traditional dark uniforms and caps have been replaced by more colourful clothes. This band wore red jackets for the Gala.

Friends and Family

Roy Handy and family at the Big Meeting.

Brenda Morris with her grandfather, Avory, at the 1950 Big Meeting. They must have been successful at the coconut shie.

A group of ladies (and one gentleman) in front of Harraton Banner in the 1950s.

Above: The Seaham Banner outside the Miners' Hall. Included are: Les Peel, Dickie Marrin, and Harold Mitchell.

Left: Lumley 6th Pit Lodge at the Gala in the 1960s. The kids are having a great time.

Gareth Wilkins, a proud Banner holder, at the 2008 Gala.

Peter Shields and wife Carol at the 2007 Gala.

Taking the weight of their feet during a long day at the 2008 Gala.

The Graham family at the 2007 Gala – Linda, Jack, Martin, Kim and Ebony.

Marching through Durham in 2008 are, left to right: Sonia Hawkins, Lynn Duke and Dave Hawkins. Lynn's dad, Bob Cutting, worked at Silksworth Colliery.

Jack Hall at the 2008 Gala. Jack worked all his life in the mines; first at Silksworth until closure in 1971 and then went to work at Wearmouth Colliery.

Memories of a Pit Boy

P.J. McPartland described his memories of growing up in a colliery community in his book 'Pit Boy – Memories of a life in Murton during the 1930s and '40s'. Here he recalls attending the Miners' Gala in its heyday:

Durham Big Meeting, as it has always been known in Murton, was a vast working-class pageant and the largest trade union gathering in the world, which could trace its origins well back into the 19th century.

Early on the morning of the big day, the lodge banner would be unfurled and paraded through the streets before departure for Durham, preceded by the colliery band, and accompanied by miners' union officials and numerous hangers-on, both the serious minded and the jovially eccentric, of whom every colliery had its quota. Prancing about in comical fashion, sometimes rigged-out like pantomime dames, they could be counted on to enliven the occasion; for the Big Meeting was never a staid affair.

The scene in Durham was unforgettable, as more than a quarter of a million people crowded the twisting thoroughfares of the old city. They pressed forward slowly but purposefully, laughing, dancing, some linking arms to form chorus lines in advance of band and banner. From Elvet Bridge up Old Elvet towards the racecourse was one tumultuous mass of seething humanity. As each banner passed before the County Hotel, and the strains of the band carried upwards, the invited guests – union leaders and Labour Party heavyweights – waved cheerily to the entourage from the balcony above. The colourful, richly symbolic, banners commonly depicted heroes of the labour movement, such as Keir Hardie and Peter Lee, and bore slogans like 'Unity is Strength'; some were draped in black, denoting that a fatality had occurred at the pit in the year leading up to the Big Meeting. It was a test of stamina for the VIP guests, for it was hours before the last lodge banner was carried aloft past the County Hotel.

Later, they would deliver their speeches before thousands on the racecourse. But politics were far from the minds of many people. Families happily picnicked on the grass, while those eager to go boating on the river joined the queues which formed by the water's edge. Many were drawn to the fairground amusements, where a Wurlitzer might be heard pounding out its cheerful notes in competition with the odd bandsman practising only feet away. For some, the rush and clamour of the gala had given over to a tranquil, worshipful mood, and they made their way to the great Norman Cathedral, which, together with Durham's ancient castle, dominated the city from the escarpment high above the Wear.

At the end of the day, the banner was brought home to Murton, and for the second time paraded through the village, an event which created a fair amount of excitement, for it

The Murton Lodge Banner showing the Conishead Priory Convalescent Home.

brought throngs of people from their houses out on to the street. 'I can hear the band!' someone would cry eagerly, while it was still some considerable way off. Then, after a few moments, 'I can see the banner!' Eyes would be strained for a glimpse of it coming into view above the heads of the crowd. In a short while, the parade would go by, the band playing a rousing march, people walking proudly in procession behind the banner, children skipping along at the side, the two men bearing the weight of the poles which supported the banner by this time feeling the strain and sweating profusely. The parade concluded with a march down the Terrace to the Miners' Hall at the bottom, where the procession disbanded, and the lodge banner was carefully put away until the next time.

Right: *The Murton Banner at the Big Meeting in 2006.*

The band leads the way for Dawdon Banner in Claypath at the 1950 Gala.

Through The Streets of Durham

Two views of the Dawdon Banner and supporters marching at the Gala in 1965. One of the men in the fancy dress is Bill Wood – well known for his costumes on Gala Day.

The Dipton Delight Banner with officials and supporters marching through Durham. At the front are the junior section – The Delight Chips – with their own banner.

The band leads the way for the Blackhall Banner at the 2008 Gala.

Gordon Sayers, dressed as a miner, with the Horden Lodge Officials at the 1965 Gala.

Remember The Good Old Days

Miner's son Arthur Curtis recalls his memories of the Gala from the late 1940s.

Christmas and birthday rolled into one and doubled! Yes, those two occasions were welcomed and exciting, but Gala Day was the day to savour with deep anticipation. It had far more elements than the regular gifts of the Rupert annual, crayons and tangerines of Christmas and clothing and Dan Dare annuals for birthdays.

This was *the* special day. The anticipation was tangible and was highlighted the day prior to the Gala Day when Mam would start cooking thin fadge loaves to be split with the meat-flavoured dripping carefully saved from the last roast and tea-cakes to be spread with butter and jam. As a helper on the day (coincidentally, I was always too ill to attend school on that Friday). I was allowed two luxuries. Wet lettuce leaves dipped in the sugar bowl and thin slices of cheese liberally spread with home-made strawberry jam.

Dad was a regular member of the team of banner carriers. To us, when he was chosen, it meant that we could walk alongside him, right under the banner and immediately behind the brass and pipe band. Great excitement of course, but it also meant that the two pounds ten he got for being a bearer paid the train fair, the rest being shared around his family. Seven and six each! So with a real fortune burning holes in our pockets we'd all assemble outside the Miners' Hall. The banner would be unfurled and lifted proudly while the band tuned up. Then we'd march with pride to the Railway Station with buses and trams piling up behind us.

We had never travelled further than Durham City in our lives so this was a once-a-year occasion in so many ways. The rhythmical pattern of sound as the train raced over the gaps in the silver lines beneath still reverberates in my mind. The station at Durham was a cacophony of noise created by bands re-tuning, parents shouting to excited kids about where to meet if they get lost. Lost? We're not lost. You just can't see us. We can see the Castle, the Cathedral, the river and the skinny cobble-stoned streets leading to the racecourse covered with canvas stalls.

The streets of Durham are packed for this Big Meeting Day in the 1950s.

The organisation must have been unbelievable. To get that many bands, banners and pitmen and their families into some semblance of order would have been horrific, but hey that wasn't even a thought to the thousands of children marching so proudly with their parents. Neither were there stops to hear political speeches. We knew what we wanted and where to get it.

We each had our own paper carrier bag of Mam's cooking and an apple or orange. We also had seven and six safely held into a pocket closed by a safety pin. Oh the mind was boggling at what we were going to buy – Walls ice cream; drinks of every variety, flavour and temperature; hot potatoes cooked in their jackets and designed to keep fingers burning and lips pursed to blow often; or whelks (pronounced 'whilecks' freshly cooked in salt water with a free pin to extract them from their shells.

Mam's fadge made a great repository for hot chips which melted the meaty dripping into the body of the bread. Ambrosia! No-one was richer or happier than us on those days. We spent our time running from one stall to the next spending as little as possible until we'd decided how best to spend a rapidly dwindling fortune lost to food stalls.

No wastage on palm-readers, fortune-tellers, instant portraits in charcoal, bearded ladies, balloons with suggestive pictures or wording, fancy hats or whatnot. Having circled the grounds we started to visit the stalls of our choosing and went our different ways. We knew where Mam and Dad would be when we exhausted our money and bodies.

Shooting galleries had the most enticing prizes and probably bent gun sights to keep the prizes for the next fair the owner visited, but who cared? It was the excitement of having money to spend and the possibility of a small, unbought souvenir of the day. The Roll-a-penny would lose you a shilling faster than it took to get the twelve coins in exchange for a bob and they never seemed to come to rest exactly inside a square labelled 'shilling' or 'half crown'.

An open mouthed clown turning 180 degrees was my favourite waste of money. You got five table tennis balls and inserted them in your own time into a mouth and the balls were disgorged into wooden walled slots with varying scores. If your total score matched any of the numbers boldly displayed by the prize, then it was yours. One glorious, unforgettable (after 50 years) Gala Day, I won a watch. It had probably cost more over the years of trying than the value of the watch itself, but I had won it.

I can't remember much of the end of those splendid days. I remember clearly reaching the grassy knoll where the family waited, but whether we marched behind bands or wandered back to the station I can't recollect. Neither can I recall the train's return to Sunderland or the bus ride back home.

What I do remember is that as a boy scout camping at Sharpley Woods we would sit around the camp fire and sing Ralph Reader songs. One included the lines: 'These are the times we shall dream about and remember the good old days.'

Thank you Mr Reader; you were a most prescient writer. Wow! Seven and six!

Originally published in Mining Memories by Andrew Clark.

Families and friends in front of the Burnhope Lodge Banner.

When Banners Were Draped In Black

In 2000, Carol Roberton of the Sunderland Echo asked readers for their memories of the Durham Miners' Gala to help people remember its importance to local culture. Former Vane Tempest miner Derek Gillum shared half a century of memories.

The Gala memories of Derek Gillum – happy times, sad times, times of protest – stretch back to 1951 when he went with his family as a child. Later, Derek, who now lives in Sunderland, marched as a miner with the Vane Tempest Banner.

He recalls the contrast in when the Brandon Banner was the first in Durham City and 300 teenagers danced through the streets behind band and banner. But the Easington contingent were sombre, their banner draped in black in memory of 83 miners who lost their lives when an explosion ripped through the pit.

In 1969, he remembers the Easington Banner was again draped in black – unexpectedly. Just the night before the gala two men were killed by a fall of stone down the pit. One had lost his father in the 1951 explosion. 'My heart went out to their families,' says Derek, originally from Silksworth.

He remembers the 1960s more clearly. 'I remember one year when our Lodge, Silksworth, had a silent protest. The band stopped playing outside the County Hotel, where Labour leaders were on the balcony, and the miners marched past in silence. This silent protest was against pit closures. It was the first time a lodge had done this. Nobody thought that a few years later our own pit would be closed with many others.'

Derek wonders if anyone remembers Mrs Louise Ramshaw who for many years was the Horden Lodge mascot and used to march dressed as a miner, or Bill Wood, John George and Tommy Hopkirk, who wore comic fancy dress as they came in with the Dawdon Banner. Derek says the last parade of the Hylton Lodge Banner was accompanied by the Coal Queen of that year, Andrea Buckley of Red House Estate, Sunderland. He remembers the moving sight of 1983 when 100 old banners were paraded for the first time in many years.

'When you look back over the past and see how many pits have gone, it makes you feel very sad. From Vesting Day to 1999, 137 pits and drifts have gone,' says Derek. 'We must keep it going for men like my father Fred, who worked 35 years underground at Ryhope and Seaham and died, aged 50, like many others who also lost their lives to the mines but are still alive in our hearts. Governments over the years have closed our pits and killed off the lifeblood of our villages, but they have not killed off the spirit of the Durham miner and the Gala. Long may it continue.'

This article was originally published in the Sunderland Echo, 3rd April 2000.

Left: Easington Lodge Banner, draped in black, passes the Royal County Hotel.

Hard Times

Maurice Ridley in the book 'Our Village – Memories of the Durham Mining Communities', by Keith Armstrong, remembers the Gala of 1926 – the time of the General Strike.

During the early weeks of the strike the Durham Miners' Gala was held. Usually, of course, the Gala is held in Durham but in 1926, for a number of reasons, it was held at Burnhope. I walked there with other young locked-out miners and our parents, and it was my first real experience of the leadership that was really in charge of our struggle. I should say that the speech of Arthur Cook, who was the secretary of the miners' union, affected me for the rest of my life.

There were at least thirty thousand miners at the meeting. It was a magnificent turnout and, of course, they had to get there the best way they could and many of them walked from goodness knows where. We walked five or six miles, but many of the people there that day walked much further. But that didn't matter. Even though it wasn't held in Durham, it was recognised that this meeting taking place at Burnhope was to be addressed by the leadership of the miners and the politicians within the labour movement who were supporting us. For any ordinary trade unionist it would have been a crime not to be able to go. I mean you just automatically had to go because you were in the midst of the struggle.

Right: The Chopwell Banner getting ready to leave the Gala field in 2006. The Chopwell miners suffered greatly during the General Strike – when it started they had already been out for 11 months after a dispute with the Consett Iron Company.

The Eppleton Lodge Banner during the 1984 Miners' Strike. The Burnhope Women's Support Group Banner is on the left.

The Justice for Mineworkers Banner for those victimised, sacked or imprisoned.

Remembering A Sad Day

Coal mining was always a dangerous industry and there were many major disasters in the Durham Coalfield. One such tragedy occurred on the 14th October 1906 when an explosion ripped through Wingate Colliery killing twenty-four pitmen.

Right: The Wingate Lodge Banner leads the funeral procession a few days after the disaster.

A century after the explosion at Wingate Colliery the local community held a Memorial Service to remember those who lost their lives. Here are a few images from that day.

The Wingate Banner draped in black is paraded through the village.

Wingate schoolchildren with their own Banner at the 2006 service.

Flowers and pit lamps laid at the Memorial in Wingate.

The Wingate Memorial Service, 14th October 2006, to remember the men and boys killed in the explosion at Wingate Colliery in 1906.

The Centenary Gala

The Big Meeting of 1983 was the centenary Gala and saw many old Banners attending that day. That year's speakers included: Neil Kinnock MP, Leader of the Labour Party, Tony Benn MP and Lawrence Daly, Secretary of the National Union of Mineworkers. Bands from Vane Tempest, Horden and Easington played at the Miners' Festival Service.

Right: The Silksworth Lodge at the Centenary Miners' Gala in 1983.

The band leads the way for the Easington Lodge Banner at the Centenary Gala.

At the 1983 Gala, Kellingley Colliery Banner, from Yorkshire, and Hedley Hope Lodge.

The Handon Hold Lodge Banner that was last paraded at the Gala in 1983.

The Thornley Banner at the 1983 Big Meeting.

Mining Memories

Right: Mr & Mrs Dave Hopper with Red Hill in the background. The Durham Miners' Association was formed in 1869 and was made up from Lodges from each colliery. In 1870 William Crawford became agent for the Association and his portrait appeared on Banners from Cornsay, Ryhope, Haswell and many others. Today, the union is run by Dave Hopper, Dave Guy, Alan Cummings and also back room staff at the headquarters at Red Hill.

Above: Greenside Colliery lamp cabin. When the pits were closed thousands of lamps were destroyed but now they are treasured collectors' items. In recent years a Banner Group set up in Greenside restored the old Banner to its former glory.

Left: Billy Middleton and his Gran at the 1951 Gala. Behind them is the Wheatley Hill Banner with a portrait of Peter Lee. Bill, who is now 67 years old, worked all his life in the mines and is the Secretary of the New Thornley Banner Group.

Silksworth Banner Group was formed in 2005 to raise funds for a new Banner. The Banner, made by the Bearpark Artist Co-op, was unfurled in 2006 at Silksworth Comrades Club by two ex-Silksworth Union men, Lawrence Robinson and Bill Border. They are standing between Eddy Donkin on unfurling night (*right*).

Robert and Eric Border at unfurling night for the Silksworth Banner.

Left: Members of Silksworth Mining Society at Willington for an exhibition in 2008. Left to right: George Kennedy (ex-Silksworth miner), Jack Graham (ex-Vane Tempest miner) and Gareth Wilkins.

Silksworth Mining Society was formed in 2004 and has held over 70 exhibitions throughout County Durham and Tyne & Wear. At their exhibitions they display photographs and mining memorabilia and help keep alive some great traditions.

A young lad called Cameron on a replica pit pony at a mining exhibition at Bowburn in 2008. Exhibitions such as this are one way young people can experience mining heritage.

Brian Scollon, Bill Lees and George Maitland at Sunderland's Stadium of Light for a celebration by the North East England Mining Archive and Research Centre. The Research Centre is based at the Murray Library in Sunderland.

Banners of Pride

The Banner almost has its own personality. Much thought is given to colour, design and size and a lot of consultation with artists and the firm that will make the Banner and bring it to life. Then comes the important day when it is unveiled.

Bradley Shop Lodge, Leadgate – a Mechanics Banner.

Deaf Hill Lodge Banner at the Gala in the 1960s.

Clara Vale Lodge Banner and supporters.

Seaham Lodge Banner at the 1994 Gala.

Fenhall Drift Lodge Banner, Lanchester in 1997. The paper on the top of the Banner says Thrislington Lodge.

New Herrington Lodge Banner in the 1990s.

Ryhope Banner at the Gala in 2005.

Houghton Lodge Banner outside the Welfare Hall in Houghton in the mid 1950s.

Witton Lodge Banner in the 1960s.

Eppleton Lodge Banner and officials in the 1970s.

Horden Banner at the 1995 Gala.

Elemore Lodge Banner in the 1960s.

Spennymoor Lodge's New Banner at the 2006 Gala.

The GMB Union Banner at the 2007 Gala.

Dawdon Lodge Banner and officials in the 1950s.

Lumley 6th Pit Banner at the 2006 Gala.

Sacriston Lodge Banner and officials.

Wearmouth Lodge Banner at the 1994 Gala.

Heading Home

At the end of the Gala, Banners and bands would go back to their villages and march back to their clubs and say it has been a great day.

South Hetton Banner on its way home from the 1950 Gala.

Coming home from the Gala, the Silksworth Banner in 2008. Gareth Wilkins is on the pole with Tony Gleghorn behind. The band are the Shepherd Band from York whose organiser is Charles Wilson.

Recent Times

Although deep coal mining has now gone from County Durham the area's rich heritage is not forgotten by the many men and women who worked in the industry. That heritage is on display in force at the Durham Miners' Gala. Long live the Gala.

Seaham Banner – one of the founding members of the DMA – at the 2006 Gala.

Herrington Lodge Banner ready to leave for home from the 2006 Gala.

Dave Hopper, General Secretary NUM Durham Area, speaking at the platform on the Racecourse in 2008.

Chilton Banner at the 2008 Gala. Volunteers raise money all year round to parade their Banner at the Gala.

Silksworth Banner waiting for the off in 2008. Gareth Wilkins and Martin Graham are on the poles. Peter Shields on the rope is Secretary of Silksworth Banner Group. Standing on the right is Ivy Gleghorn.

At the 2008 Gala, the Silksworth Lodge Banner with the Shepherd Band from York.

Supporters with Ryhope's Banner at the 2007 Gala.

Washington F Pit Lodge Banner at the 2008 Gala.

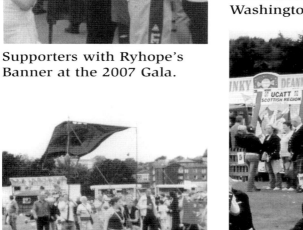

A Banner making its way home in 2006.

Lumley 6th Pit Banner at the 2008 Gala.

Wingate Lodge Banner at the 2006 Gala.

Dawdon Lodge Banner with pipe band at the 2008 Gala. Their Banner Group is run by John Parkin.

Acknowledgements

The author would like to thank the following who have helped with this book:

Alan Cummings (Easington Lodge); Jack, Linda, Martin, Kim & Ebony Graham, George Kennedy, Peter and Carol Shields, Gareth Wilkins, Alan McAdo, Ian Brewster, Andrew Clark, Joe Davision (Silksworth Mining Society and Banner Group); Brian Scollon (Seaham historian); George Maitland (Murton History Group), Roy Lambeth, Bill Middleton (New Thornley Banner Group); DMA David Hopper and staff; David Gillum, Jean Gillum; Alan Jones; Ron Gray (mining artist); Phil & Emma Blakey; Jack Hall; Paul & Lynn Duke; Keith Armstrong; P.J. McPartland; Arthur Curtis; Ray Card; George Nairn; Tom Hutchinson; Tom Bainbridge; Lena Cooper; Jack Hair, Alan Harrison & Hylton Marrs; Olive Linge; Jim Pace; Alan Brett; Francis & Margaret Newman (Sunniside Local History Society); Carol Roberton, Sunderland Echo; Owen McGuire; Bill Lees; Pat Simmons (Lambton & Houghton Banner Group); Marjorie Rowe, Howard, Katherine, Craig & Anna Ward; Ashley Sutherland (Sunderland Local Studies); Silksworth RAOB, Silksworth British Legion & Silksworth Comrades.

The book is in memory of Dicky Briggs who was born at Silksworth and worked at the local pit. Dicky lived most of his life in the village but left to go in the RAF where he served as a radar operator. Dicky was a good footballer and played for West Auckland who many years before were winners of the Sir Thomas Lipton Trophy (the first the World Cup) in 1909 and 1911. Dickie was in the side that played at Wembley in the FA Amateur Cup in 1961 when they were defeated by Walthamstow Avenue. The people of Silksworth will not forget the feisty left winger. *Above*: The West Auckland team Dicky played for. He is sitting far left.

Also available from Summerhill Books

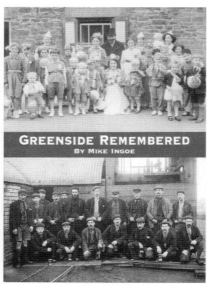

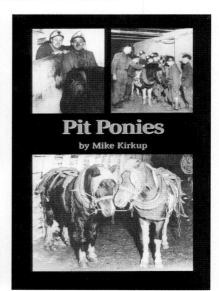

Thanks For The Memories
(Fence Houses, Lambton, Burnmoor, Chilton Moor, Dubmire & Bankhead)

Greenside Remembered
(Over 300 photographs remember this former mining community)

Pit Ponies
(The story of pit ponies in the Northumberland and Durham Coalfields)